IRAN
the land

April Fast

A Bobbie Kalman Book

The Lands, Peoples, and Cultures Series

Crabtree Publishing Company
www.crabtreebooks.com

The Lands, Peoples, and Cultures Series

Created by Bobbie Kalman

Author: April Fast
Third edition: Q2AMedia
Editor: Adrianna Morganelli
Content and Photo editor: Kokila Manchanda
Editorial director: Kathy Middleton
Production coordinator: Margaret Salter
Prepress technician: Margaret Salter
Project manager: Kumar Kanul
First and second editions
    Coordinating editor: Ellen Rodger
    Project editor: Rachel Eagen
    Production coordinator: Rosie Gowsell
    Project development: First Folio Resource Group, Inc.
    Photo research: Maria DeCambra
    Consultants: Dr. Mehrangiz Nikou, Dr. Maria O'Shea

Illustrations:
Dianne Eastman: icon
David Wysotski, Allure Illustrations: back cover

Map:
Jim Chernishenko

Icon: *Badgirs*, or wind towers, appear at the head of each section. They stand on the roofs of homes in the desert city of Yazd. For most of the year, the *badgirs* catch cool breezes and direct them into the homes. During winter, they are closed off so that warm air inside does not escape.

Every effort has been made to obtain the appropriate credit and full copyright clearance for all images in this book. Any oversights, despite Crabtree's greatest precautions, will be corrected in future editions.

Photographs:
AFP: Atta Kenare: p. 13 (bottom), p. 28 (bottom)
AGE/ firstlight.ca: Bruno Morandi: p. 23 (top)
Alamy: Patker Photo Agency: title page
Art Directors: Michal Cerny: p. 4, p. 6, p. 16, p. 17 (top), p. 18 (right), p. 30 (top); John Ellard: p. 26 (top); Foto Werbung: p. 9, p. 27 (top); Moshen Rastani:p. 27 (bottom); Chris Rennie: p. 8 (top); Trip: p. 20 (left)
Art Resource, NY: Erich Lessing: p. 25 (top)
Associated Media Group: Peter Langer: p. 18 (left)
Ateshkadeh, Firuzabad, Iran/www.bridgeman.co.uk: p. 25 (bottom)
Corbis: Paul Almasy: p. 5 (bottom left); Arthur Thévenart: p. 21, p. 23 (bottom); Brian A. Vikander: p. 7, p. 10 (top), p. 12 (left); Roger Wood: p. 12 (right), p. 13 (top), p. 19; Michael S. Yamashita: p. 11 (top), p. 14; Ferda Caglayan/Atlas Geographic: p. 20 (right); p. 22 (bottom), p. 24 (both); Michael Nicholson: p. 3; David A. Northcott: p. 31 (top); Earl Kowall: p. 8 (bottom); Kaveh Kazemi: p. 15 (bottom); Shepard Sherbell: p. 28 (top)
Dave Taylor: p. 30 (bottom)
Desmond Harney/ Robert Harding: p. 11 (bottom)
Lonely Planet Images: Chris Mellor: p. 22 (top)
Magnum Photos: Abbas: p. 15 (top), p. 26 (bottom)
NHPA: Daniel Heuclin: p. 31 (bottom)
Photolibrary: Dave Bartruff: p. 5 (top); P Narayan: p. 5 (center); Robert Harding: p. 10, p. 29; Mark Daffey: cover
Reuters: Morteza Nikoubazl: p.17 (bottom)

Cover: Khorramabad, the capital city of Lorestan province in Iran, spreads out at the foot of the Zagros Mountains.

Title page: Homes in the village of Kandovan, in northwestern Iran, are built into the cliffside. People have lived in Kandovan for more than 1,400 years.

Back cover: The *gandar*, or Iranian crocodile, grows to be ten to thirteen feet (three to four meters) long. In winter, it floats in rivers or basks in the sun. In summer, it lies in mud that forms at the bottom of rivers that dry out in the heat.

Library and Archives Canada Cataloguing in Publication

Fast, April, 1968-
    Iran : the land / April Fast. -- Rev. ed.

(Lands, peoples, and cultures series)
Includes index.
ISBN 978-0-7787-9276-5 (bound).--ISBN 978-0-7787-9646-6 (pbk.)

    1. Iran--Description and travel--Juvenile literature.
I. Title. II. Series: Lands, peoples, and cultures series

DS259.2.F38 2010   j955   C2009-905127-3

Library of Congress Cataloging-in-Publication Data

Fast, April, 1968-
    Iran. The land / April Fast. -- Rev. ed.
        p. cm. -- (The lands, peoples, and cultures series)
    Includes index.
    ISBN 978-0-7787-9646-6 (pbk. : alk. paper) -- ISBN 978-0-7787-9276-5 (reinforced library binding : alk. paper)
    1. Iran--Geography--Juvenile literature. I. Title. II. Series.

DS254.9.F375 2010
955--dc22

2009034285

Crabtree Publishing Company

www.crabtreebooks.com   1-800-387-7650

Printed in China/122009/CT20090915

Published in Canada
Crabtree Publishing
616 Welland Ave.
St. Catharines, ON
L2M 5V6

Published in the United States
Crabtree Publishing
350 Fifth Ave.,
59th Floor
New York, NY 10118

Published in the United Kingdom
Crabtree Publishing
Maritime House
Basin Road North, Hove
BN41 1WR

Published in Australia
Crabtree Publishing
386 Mt. Alexander Rd.
Ascot Vale (Melbourne)
VIC 3032

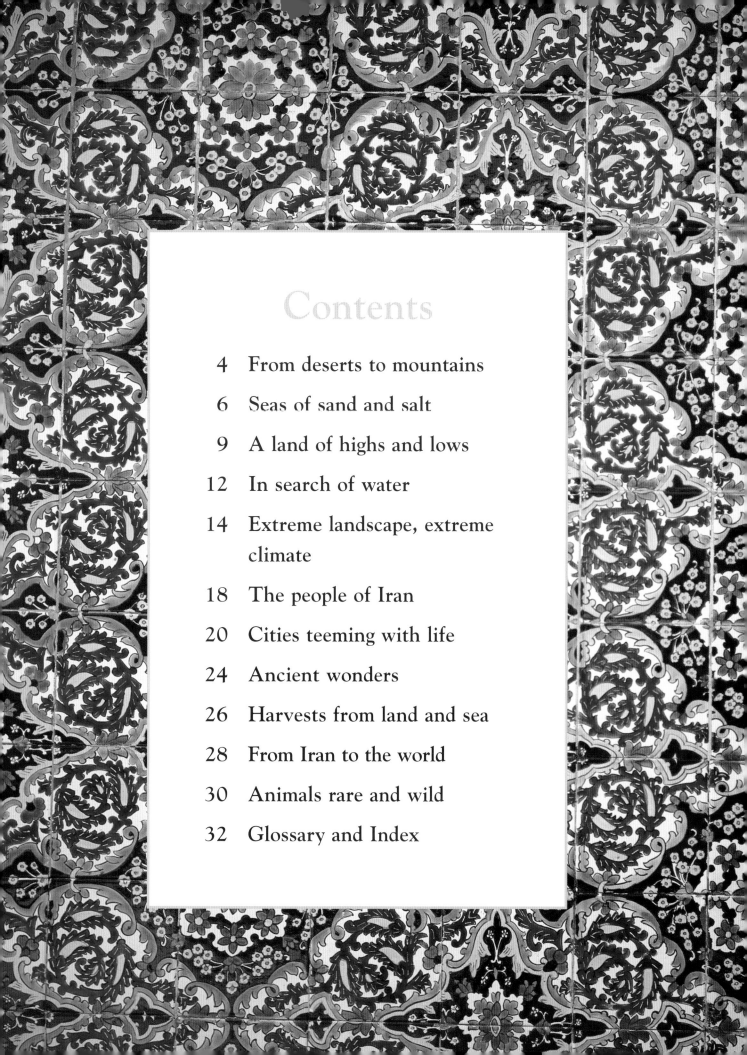

Contents

🏛 From deserts to mountains 🏛

According to an ancient Persian legend, the rain god Tistar caused rain to fall to the earth. Seas arose from the rain, then split to create seven *keshvar*, or countries. The central *keshvar*, called Khvanirath, was larger than all the others. There, the first mountain, Mount Elburz, grew from roots in the ground, and the first man and woman grew from a rhubarb plant. This is how Iran and the Iranians came to be.

The land that was Persia

The country of Iran, which was once called Persia, lies at the easternmost edge of the Middle East. The Middle East is a region that borders the southern and eastern shores of the Mediterranean Sea. Iran is roughly bowl-shaped, with a vast central **plateau** surrounded by high mountains. About one-fifth of the land is desert, but the country also contains forests, wetlands, seacoasts, and sandy island beaches.

Iran has been at the heart of many great **empires** in its history. Each one left its stamp on the land. Beautiful cities, with **mosques**, palaces, and bazaars, or street markets, were built. **Irrigation** systems were constructed so that farmers could grow crops on land that was extremely dry and prone to dust storms. The land was mined for copper, gemstones, and oil, which is now Iran's most valuable **export**.

(top) Iran's territory includes islands in the Persian Gulf. Hormoz Island was once a bustling trading center, with more than 40,000 people. Today, less than 4,000 Iranians live on this island, which has sandy beaches, low cliffs, and lagoons near the shore. Further inland are plains with small hills.

(left) The Gate of All Nations stood at the entrance to the ancient city of Persepolis. The gate led to an audience hall, where the king received visitors who brought him gifts.

(below) Cotton, fish, caviar, and crude oil are exported from the port city of Bandar-e Anzali on the Caspian Sea.

Rebuilding the country

Iran suffered greatly during a war fought in the 1980s with its western neighbor, Iraq. Many villages, cities, and oil fields were damaged, and hundreds of thousands of people were killed. Also beginning in 1979, conflicts between the governments of the United States and Iran led the United States to limit trade with Iran. This damaged Iran's **economy**. Today, Iranians are working to rebuild their economy and improve their relationships with neighboring countries and nations in the west.

Facts at a glance
Official name: Jomhuri-ye Eslami-ye Iran (Islamic Republic of Iran)
Area: 636,296 square miles (1,648,000 square kilometers)
Population: 70,495,782
Capital city: Tehran
Official language: Persian
Currency: Iranian rial
National holiday: Republic Day (April 1)

(left) A student reads outside the Shahid Motahari Mosque in the capital city of Tehran. The mosque is both a house of prayer and a school for religious studies.

5

🏛 Seas of sand and salt 🏛

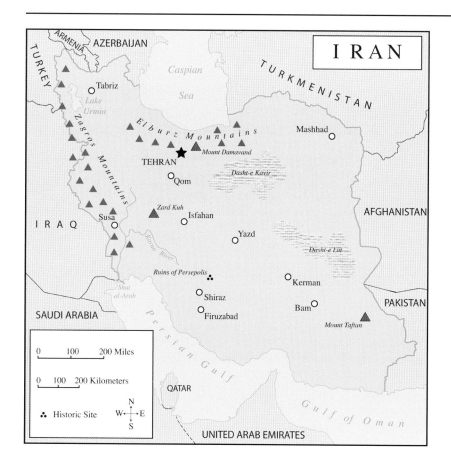

Many countries and bodies of water border Iran. To the north are Armenia, Azerbaijan, the Caspian Sea, and Turkmenistan; to the south are the Gulf of Oman and the Persian Gulf. Afghanistan and Pakistan lie to the east, while Iraq and Turkey lie to the west.

Iran's plateau

The most dominating feature of Iran's landscape is a flat plateau located in the middle of the country. The plateau is broken up by a few small mountain ranges and two enormous deserts. The salt-encrusted Dasht-e Kavir is found in northcentral Iran, and the sand-and-pebble Dasht-e Lut sits in the southeast.

(top) Only sparse vegetation, such as thorny shrubs, grows among the sand dunes in Iran's deserts.

Dasht-e Kavir

Millions of years ago, a body of water called the Sea of Tethys covered Iran's central plateau. Over time, the sea dried up, leaving behind a layer of salt. Part of this area became known as the Dasht-e Kavir, or Great Salt Desert. Deep, quicksand-like marshes called *kavirs* hide beneath the crusty salt surface. Just like thin ice over water, the salt over *kavirs* can crack open with the weight of a person or animal. This makes travel in the Dasht-e Kavir extremely dangerous. The only people in the region live on hills separating *kavirs*, in oases, and in the surrounding mountains.

Dasht-e Lut

The Dasht-e Lut is believed to be one of the hottest and driest places in the world. Enormous sand dunes lie in its east. In the west are high mountain ridges separated by windswept valleys. The Dasht-e Lut also has dried-out *kavirs* and a large salt marsh.

Salt plugs

Salt plugs, also called salt domes or diapirs, are circular masses of salt with rounded tops. They stand up to 4,000 feet (1,200 meters) tall and three miles (five kilometers) wide. Over time, tectonic activity, which causes the land to shift and shake, forces salt plugs to erupt from deep within the earth. More than two hundred of these pinkish-white or yellowish masses are found in the southern Zagros region of Iran. Scientists believe some of the salt plugs are millions of years old.

Few people live in this desert, except along the eastern rim, where a small amount of rain falls, and in the west, where water from nearby mountain slopes soaks into the ground, making farming possible.

In the 1600s, caravans of merchants traveling in the dry, hot Dasht-e Lut stopped for food and shelter at a caravansary, or inn, called Zein-o-Din. Only the remains of Zein-o-Din can be seen today.

Oases

Oases are **fertile** areas located around the edges of the desert plateau. They occur in places where water trapped underground comes close to the surface through faults, or cracks, in the earth's rock layer. In some oases, groundwater forms springs or pools on the surface. In the past, **nomadic** peoples and trade **caravans** stopped at oases to rest and drink. Many of Iran's oases developed into large cities, such as Isfahan, Shiraz, Yazd, and Qom, which have been inhabited for thousands of years.

Palm trees in an oasis near the southeastern city of Bam.

Desert taxis

Iran's nomadic and **semi-nomadic** peoples, who make up ten percent of the population, travel between their *yilaqs*, or summer locations, and *qeshlaqs*, or winter locations, in search of food and water for their herds. They use pack animals, such as horses, mules, and camels, to carry their belongings. Camels, which are nicknamed "ships of the desert," can survive for long periods without water or food. They have wide, tough feet that spread over the sand, so they do not sink, and nostrils that close tightly against flying sand.

Camels are not only used as pack animals. Their wool is made into clothing and tents; their dung is used to fuel fires; and once they die, their hides are made into shoes and saddles.

The village of Masuleh sits 3,445 feet (1,050 meters) high on a cliff in the Elburz Mountains.

A land of highs and lows

Iran's central plateau is almost completely surrounded by rugged mountains. Throughout history, people have traveled with pack animals through passes, or gaps, in the mountains to reach the plateau. Today, paved roads and railways have made traveling easier.

Mountains

Iran's main mountain system, the Zagros Mountains, stretches for more than 1,000 miles (1,600 kilometers) from northwest to southeast. The tallest peak in the Zagros, Zard Kuh, rises 14,918 feet (4,547 meters) high. Some people, including many nomadic groups, live in the Zagros, farming in fertile areas.

Deep rivers cut through the landscape in the north, while fertile plains separate the mountain ridges in the south.

The Elburz Mountains are a steep, narrow range bordering the Caspian Sea. Iran's highest peak, Mount Damavand, stands 18,602 feet (5,670 meters) tall in the central part of the Elburz. The snowy caps of Mount Damavand loom majestically above Iran's capital, Tehran. The Talish Mountains are a smaller chain connected to the Elburz. They are found in the northwestern and western parts of the country.

(top left) Rivers rushing through the Zagros Mountains cut deep canyons into the landscape.

Volcanoes

Two volcanic regions lie in northwestern Iran, while a third stretches from Azerbaijan, in the northwest, to Baluchistan, a province in the southeast. Most of Iran's volcanoes have been inactive for hundreds of years, but Mount Taftan, in the southeast, erupted in 1993. No damage was reported, but the volcano still spews mud and hot gas.

Predicting volcanoes

Scientists predict volcanic activity by watching for small earthquakes and vibrations near a volcano. These are caused by the movement of hot liquid rock, called magma, in the earth's core. As magma moves closer to the earth's surface, it causes a volcano to swell. Swelling, along with fumaroles, indicates that a volcano might be ready to erupt.

Mount Damavand, in the Elburz Mountains, is a volcano with fumaroles. Fumaroles are small holes that release steam and strong fumes that smell of sulfur.

Hot springs

Hot springs bubble mainly near the Caspian Sea and in the volcanic areas of the northwest. The springs form when underground water is heated by pressure at great depths or by hot volcanic rock near the surface. The water then rises to the surface through cracks in the earth and forms pools of hot water. Some people believe that bathing in these waters, which are filled with **minerals** and salts, can cure illnesses such as back pain, stomach problems, and a painful swelling of the joints called arthritis.

Lowlands

Iran's lowland areas lie in the southwest and the north. The Khuzestan plain, in the southwest, rises only a few feet above sea level as it stretches from the Persian Gulf to the foothills of the Zagros Mountains. The plain, which is about 75 miles (120 kilometers) wide, is covered with saltwater **mangrove** swamps along the coast and freshwater marshes farther inland.

The Caspian plain, in the north, is 1.2 miles (two kilometers) wide in some spots to 70 miles (115 kilometers) wide in others. Sand dunes close to the shore give way inland to lagoons, marshlands, and forests. The Caspian forest, also called the Hyrcanian forest, is a tropical woodland of walnut, maple, teakwood, and olive trees. Much of the forest has been cleared to make way for farms where rice, fruit, cotton, and tea are grown.

(above) Water from hot springs flows down a channel, or qanat, in the south. The water is used for washing and for crop irrigation.

(below) Lowlands at the foot of Iran's mountains are made fertile by the water that flows down mountain rivers and streams.

11

⚜ In search of water ⚜

Iran's border is nearly one-half coastline and includes the Caspian Sea, Persian Gulf, and Gulf of Oman. In spite of all the water that surrounds Iran, there is little water within the country. There are several small saltwater lakes, the largest of which is Lake Urmia in the northwest. It is swampy and too salty to sustain fish or most other forms of aquatic life. A few small freshwater lakes, created by melting snow and rainfall, lie in high mountain valleys.

Shallow waters

Most of Iran's rivers begin in the mountains. In spring, when it rains and snow begins to melt, mountain rivers can become rushing waterways. Many rivers flow out to the seas, while others flow out to the deserts, where they dry up in the extreme heat. The only river large enough for ships to travel on is the Karun. It begins in the southwestern Zagros Mountains, then flows into the Shatt al-Arab River, and on to the Persian Gulf.

Bridges spanning the Dez River, a branch of the Karun, have collapsed because of the force of the rushing water in spring.

The Qezal Owson River flows through a valley in the Elburz Mountains. Dams, development, and pollution in the river are endangering sturgeon, a type of fish whose eggs are a delicacy called caviar.

Fighting over water

The Shatt al-Arab River runs 120 miles (193 kilometers) from southeastern Iraq to the Persian Gulf. The last 45 miles (72 kilometers) of the river form a natural border between Iraq and Iran. Until 1975, the Iran-Iraq border lay at the Iranian shoreline, which meant that Iraq had control of the entire waterway. In 1975, an agreement called the Algiers Accord moved the border halfway across the river, which gave the countries equal access to the waterway.

In 1980, Iraq went to war against Iran, partly because it wanted complete control over the Shatt al-Arab. The war lasted eight years, but did not change the location of the border. Today, both Iran and Iraq dam the river to create **reservoirs** or to redirect the flow of water for irrigation. Each country believes that the other is using more than its fair share of water. In a region known for its dryness, careful water use is a serious issue.

(left) The Mohammad Reza Shah Dam, built into a narrow canyon in western Iran, helps irrigatethe surrounding land and is a source of hydroelectricity, or water power.

Irrigating the land

Since ancient times, Iranians have used rivers to water the land. In some areas, water flows down from the mountains and seeps underground. Farmers dig wells to tap into this water. Other areas require irrigation: water must be redirected from lakes, rivers, or oases to farmlands, towns, and cities so that crops can be watered, and people and animals have water to drink.

Qanats

Qanats are long man-made tunnels that bring water from underground **aquifers** up to the surface. *Qanats* begin high in the mountains and end in lower areas, so the water flows by gravity. This method of irrigation was developed in Iran around 500 B.C. and is still used throughout the country. *Qanats* are ideal for Iran's hot, dry climate because they protect the water from the sun's heat and prevent **evaporation**.

(above) Water courses through some cities and villages in open channels called jubs, where children sometimes cool off. It was once common for water from jubs to be directed to abanbars, or storage spaces in the basements of homes. The water was used for washing. Drinking water was delivered by horse-drawn vehicles in cities, or was obtained from structures, also called abanbars, where water from qanats was stored.

🏛 Extreme landscape, extreme climate 🏛

Iran's landscape varies greatly in elevation, **latitude**, and nearness to seas or mountains. As a result, the country experiences a wide range of temperatures.

The area around Tehran, just south of the Caspian plain, has hot summers and cool winters, with temperatures as low as 30° Fahrenheit (–1° Celsius). In the central plateau, summers are hotter and drier, while winters stay mild, often a comfortable 68° Fahrenheit (20° Celsius). Southern Iran is searingly hot and humid in the summer, with daytime temperatures often reaching 122° Fahrenheit (50° Celsius).

In the desert
For most of the year, the deserts of central Iran are extremely hot. Traditional homes in the desert city of Yazd have tall wind towers called *badgirs* that channel fresh breezes inside. Underground rooms provide a cool living space, while rooftops are ideal for sleeping at night.

(top) Badgirs, *or wind tunnels, such as those in Yazd, are often open on all sides to catch the breezes, no matter which direction they are blowing.*

(above) Riders slide down a snowy hill on tires.

In the mountains

Iran's mountain communities have snow in winter and comfortable summer weather. The Zagros Mountains have severe winters, with average daily temperatures dropping below freezing. Summers in the Zagros are warm, averaging 77° Fahrenheit (25° Celsius) in the northwest and 91° Fahrenheit (33° Celsius) in the central and southern parts. More than 11 inches (280 millimeters) of rain and snow fall annually, mainly between October and April.

(below) A group of women enjoy themselves at a public beach in Alamdeh, located on the shores of the Caspian Sea in north Iran.

Around the Caspian Sea

The fringe of land between the Caspian Sea and Elburz Mountains is hot and humid in summer, with average temperatures of 100° Fahrenheit (38° Celsius). Winters are mild, with rare frost.

The subtropical climate is caused by warm winds from the Caspian that are forced to rise where they meet the mountains. The air cools as it rises. Since cool air cannot hold much water, the moisture is squeezed out. This creates a humid environment that supports jungle-like growth. Up to 78 inches (1,980 millimeters) of rain falls annually on the Caspian plain. Houses in this region are therefore raised on short wooden or concrete piles, or posts, to prevent rot and flooding.

Rushing water

Surprisingly, in a land as dry as Iran, floods are a dangerous threat. When snow-capped mountains thaw in spring, streams and rivers swell. The water rushes toward lowland areas, destroying mountain passes and bridges, and blocking routes used by nomadic peoples. Flooding also washes out railroads for days at a time and destroys crops. One of the main areas of flooding is in the Khuzestan plain in the southwest where five streams meet.

Droughts

Although some parts of Iran suffer from floods, the dry plateau areas of central, eastern, and southern Iran experience drought, or long periods when little or no rain falls. In 1999 and 2000, southern Iran suffered the country's worst drought in 30 years. People living in the region were without clean drinking water, *qanats* dried up, lakes shriveled into puddles of mud, crops withered, and wildlife suffered.

(top) Mountain streams flow heavy after spring rains. The flow of the water lessens in summer as temperatures become hotter and the air becomes drier.

Summer winds

During Iranian summers, two seasonal winds blow through the land. The *Shomal* blows from the northwest and the *Seistan*, or Wind of 120 Days, blows from the north. Both winds reach speeds of up to 70 miles (117 kilometers) per hour and often bring drought, severe heat, and sand and dust storms.

Sand and dust storms

Normally, the roots of plants anchor soil, but when the land is barren, as in the desert, fine soil particles are easily blown into the air. Sand storms occur when Iran's strong winds cause grains of sand to bounce up and down, bump into one another, then form clouds close to the ground. In dust storms, dust and tiny pieces of silt are blown high into the air, reaching an average height of 4,500 feet (1,370 meters). The desert also experiences eddies on hot afternoons, when strongly heated air near the ground rises and creates funnel-shaped dust clouds.

Damage from storms

Both the *Shomal* and the *Seistan* damage houses, and flying dust and sand scrape skin, get into the eyes of people and animals, and cause breathing problems. People are warned to stay home to avoid injury during these storms. Dust and sand also get into vehicles and machinery, wearing away at glass and wires.

On shaky ground

Iran is one of the world's most earthquake-prone countries. Many small earthquakes shake the land each year, and every so often, a major earthquake causes a great deal of damage and many deaths. Iran has many fault lines, or places where the rocky plates that make up the earth's crust meet. The fault lines are mainly along the western border and in the northeast. When the plates move along a fault line, they create vibrations that cause buildings to collapse, bridges to snap, mountains to rise,and the ground to fall or, in some cases, to spiit open.

(above) Riverbeds completely dry out in the stifling temperatures of the Dasht-e Lut.

Quake-proofing

In 1989, many Iranian cities adopted a set of rules to prevent devastation from earthquakes. Mud-brick walls must now have support beams to prevent them from collapsing. Builders must also use hollow concrete bricks to minimize damage, and concrete roofs, stone **foundations**, and steel corner pillars to add strength and flexibility to structures.

(above) The people of the ancient city of Bam begin to rebuild their homes after a devastating earthquake in December 2003. The earthquake destroyed much of the city and killed more than 40,000 people.

♔ The people of Iran ♔

(above) Men of Persian descent often wear turbans as a headcovering.

Iran is home to a diverse mix of people, including Persians, Turks, Kurds, and Arabs. Most Iranians are Muslims, or people who follow the religion of Islam. Muslims believe in one God. "God" is "Khoda" in Persian and "Allah" in Arabic, the language of the *Qur'an*, the Muslim holy book. Muslims also follow the teachings of prophets, who they believe deliver messages from God. The last Muslim prophet was Muhammad. Small numbers of Iranians also follow the religions of Zoroastrianism, Judaism, Christianity, and Baha'ism.

Persians

Persians make up about half of Iran's population. They are **descendants** of the many peoples who once ruled Iran, including the Aryan Persians, who first settled in the central plateau around 1300 B.C. Most Iranians of Persian descent follow a branch of Islam called Shi'i Islam. They speak Persian, which they call Farsi, the official language of Iran.

(right) Approximately 1,714,000 Qashqais live in Iran. Some have settled in villages and cities, while others are nomadic or semi-nomadic. They move with their herds of sheep and goats between summer pastures in the mountains and winter pastures in the foothills.

Turkic peoples

Twenty-five percent of Iran's population is made up of Turkic peoples. The largest group are the Azari people. Most Azaris live in the Azerbaijan region of northwestern Iran or in Tehran. Their language is Azari, and most are Shia Muslims. Other Turkic peoples in Iran include the Qashqais, who live around the south central city of Shiraz, and the Turkmen, who live in the northeastern province of Khorasan.

Kurds

An estimated five million Kurds live in Iran, especially in the Zagros Mountains, near the Iraq and Turkey borders. A traditionally nomadic people, most Kurds now farm the land or work in cities, often living in difficult conditions. The environment is harsh, and the region has become crowded with **refugees** from neighboring countries.

Regardless of where they live, Kurds are likely to dress in their traditional clothing. Men wear baggy pants, wide belts called sashes, and fringed turbans, and women wear long, flowing dresses in glittery fabrics, baggy pants, and velvet jackets. Kurds follow a branch of Islam called Sunni Islam, and speak the Kurdish language.

(top) Bakhtiari clothing protects the people from extreme weather. Bakhtiari men wear long tunics with a cloth belt and loose pants. The women wear skirts with many layers, along with shirts, vests, shawls, scarfs, and wraps.

Arabs

Arabs make up two percent of Iran's population. They are descended from the Arabs who conquered Iran in 649 A.D., bringing with them the religion of Islam. Most Arabs in Iran are Shia Muslims, and their language is Arabic. They live in the southwestern province of Khuzestan, as well as on the Iranian islands of the Persian Gulf.

Lurs and Bakhtiaris

Lurs live mainly in the mountains of Lorestan, a province in western Iran. Bakhtiaris, who are closely related to Lurs, also live in the west. Some Lurs and Bakhtiaris are nomadic or semi-nomadic, living in villages in the winter and traveling to mountain pastures in the summer with their herds of sheep and goats. Many others work in towns and cities in the construction and textile industries or in government positions. Most Lurs and Bakhtiaris are Shia Muslims, and they speak Luri, a language that is a mixture of Persian and Kurdish.

⛫ Cities teeming with life ⛫

Iran's first cities developed along trade routes established by nomadic peoples and merchants from distant lands. Many of these cities were destroyed by invaders, but were rebuilt as the cities that stand today.

Tehran

Iran's capital and largest city, Tehran, is located in the north. It was built in the 1200s, after invaders from the northeast called Mongols destroyed the nearby capital, Rey. It began as a small village but grew in size and prosperity when Agha Mohammad Khan, leader of the Qajar **Dynasty**, made it his capital in 1786.

Today, Tehran is the center of government, business, and manufacturing. The northern part of the city is modern, with office buildings, theaters, restaurants, hotels, and shopping centers, while the southern part is filled with old bazaars and historic buildings. One of Tehran's most impressive buildings is the Sepahsalar Mosque, also known as the Motahari Mosque, with its eight minarets covered in yellow and blue tiles. Golestan Palace was once the official residence of the royal family. Today, it is a museum, with halls and terraces decorated with mirrorwork, paintings, wood carvings, and marble thrones.

(left) Tehran sits in the foothills of the Elburz Mountains. The name of this capital city means "warm place" in Old Persian.

(below) The Azadi Tower, whose name means "freedom," was built in Tehran in 1971 to celebrate the 2,500th anniversary of the first Persian rulers.

Isfahan

Isfahan is in central Iran, on the banks of the Zayandeh River. It stands 5,200 feet (1,300 meters) above sea level, where the Zagros Mountains gradually give way to the desert. Isfahan is at least 2,500 years old, but reached the height of its glory as the capital of the Safavid Dynasty, which ruled Iran from 1501 to 1736. By the late 1600s, Isfahan had approximately 270 public baths, 1,800 caravansaries to shelter travelers, 50 *madrasahs*, or religious colleges, and 160 mosques.

In the 1920s, many of Isfahan's historical buildings were restored and an industrial area was built. Isfahan became a manufacturing center, as well as a center for the production of rugs, brasswork, and other handicrafts. Isfahan also has the largest bazaar in the country, called the Bazar-e Bozorg.

Tabriz

Tabriz, in the northwest, lies in a valley surrounded by hills on three sides. The city is believed to have been first settled in 300 A.D. Earthquakes have destroyed Tabriz many times, including twice in the 1700s when more than 80,000 people were killed; yet some beautiful ancient buildings remain. The Arg-e Tabriz, or Ark, is a large brick fortress built in the early 1300s. Masjed-e Kabud, or "The Blue Mosque," was built between 1465 and 1466. Intricate blue tilework adorns the building, and 55-foot (17-meter) columns are inscribed with the names of Shia holy leaders in a decorative handwriting called calligraphy.

(below) Eleven bridges span the Zayandeh River, which flows through Isfahan. The Khaju Bridge was built around 1650 as a dam. Locks in the lower of the bridge's two levels control the flow of water.

(above) Beyond the city of Tabriz is Mount Sahand, where people hike and mountain climb in the summer and ski in the winter.

(above) Shops and houses surround the golden-domed Holy Shrine of religious leader Imam Reza in Mashhad.

Mashhad

Mashhad is located in the northeast, in the Kashaf River valley, where wheat, grapes, rice, barley, oats, melons, and vegetables are grown. It is the second-largest city in Iran. Mashhad is an important **pilgrimage** site, as it houses the shrine of a beloved religious leader Imam Reza. A shrine is a place dedicated to a holy person who has died. Imam Reza's shrine complex includes prayer halls, reception rooms, offices, and a mosque, which was built in the early 1400s.

Shiraz

Shiraz, in the southwestern Zagros Mountains, was the capital of the Zand Dynasty, which ruled from 1750 to 1779. Located in a farming valley, it has long been famous for its grapes and wine. Many of Shiraz's beautiful buildings were constructed in the late 1700s. They include the Masjed-e Vakil, or Regent Mosque, which has an impressive entranceway adorned with floral panels, and the Vakil Bazaar, where the work of jewelers, carpetmakers, potters, and furniture makers is still sold today. Shiraz is also the burial place of two famous Iranian poets, Sa'di, who lived in the 1200s, and Hafiz, who lived in the 1300s. Their tombs are surrounded by gardens of fragrant flowers, cypress, and orange trees.

(above) The Nasir-ol-Molk Mosque, in Shiraz, is known for its beautiful architecture and intricate tilework.

Yazd

Yazd, located between the Dasht-e Kavir and the Dasht-e Lut deserts, is one of the oldest cities in the world. It is known for the wind towers, or *badgirs*, built on its houses and for the beautiful weavings created by its craftspeople. Yazd is also the original home of the Zoroastrian religion. Zoroastrians believe in an all-powerful god called Ahura Mazda. Ahura Mazda is represented by fire, which Zoroastrians believe he created. A holy fire enclosed in the Zoroastrian temple in Yazd is believed to have burned continuously since 470 B.C. It is tended by temple priests and protected from the public by glass.

(right) This mosque in Yazd was once part of a large complex that included a mausoleum, or building in which people are buried; a public bath; a caravansary, or inn; and a takieh, a special theater where religious plays were performed.

23

☖ Ancient wonders ☖

The remains of cities built long ago are scattered across Iran, excavated, or dug up, by **archaeologists** or still buried under layers of sand and dust. In the past, historians and archaeologists removed **artifacts** from historical sites for display in museums worldwide. Other artifacts and monuments were stolen or destroyed by war and the harsh environment. Over the past few years, the government of Iran has begun to restore its ancient wonders. It is also educating the public about the importance of protecting treasures from the past.

Persepolis

The remains of the ancient city of Persepolis, or Parsa, are located in a remote, mountainous region of southwestern Iran. Within the city's high walls were royal palaces, audience halls, and a treasury, where gold, silver, and other riches were stored. The Apadana was the largest building in Persepolis. Great receptions were held there, including ceremonies for the Persian New Year.

(top) The tombs of King Darius I, who ruled from 552 to 486 B.C., and of three later rulers are cut into the cliffs at Naqsh-e Rostam, in southwestern Iran.

(above) King Darius I made Persepolis the capital of the Persian Empire around 522 B.C. The city's remains lay buried under sand and dust until archaeologists began an extensive dig in the 1930s.

Susa

Susa, known today as Shush, is located at the foot of the Zagros Mountains, in southwestern Iran. It is one of the oldest cities in the world, with ruins that date back to 5000 B.C. A fortress once stood on the site. It honored Manishtusu, a king from the nearby region of Akkad who took control of Iran's silver mines more than 4,000 years ago. The palace of King Darius I as well as homes where the king's officials and where craftspeople once lived were also found at the site.

Firuzabad

The remains of the old city of Firuzabad are located in Fars province, in southcentral Iran. The circular city, which was first called Gur, was built between 200 and 300 A.D. by King Ardashir I. King Ardashir I had vowed to build a city on the site where he conquered his enemy, Artabanus V. He surrounded the city with a mud-brick wall that had gates to the north, south, east, and west. The Qal'eh-e Dokhtar was a three-story fort that sat atop a rocky hill. Downstream was the main palace, topped by a beautiful dome. Sunlight entered the dome through a window cut into the center.

(above) *Archers marching in a procession are depicted in this stone carving at the palace of King Darius I in Susa.*

(above) Remains of a domed hall from the palace of King Ardashir I can still be seen in Firuzabad.

Farming is one of the most important economic activities in Iran, even though the majority of the land is difficult to cultivate. To make their work easier and more affordable, many farmers form cooperatives, groups whose members share knowledge, the costs of equipment and crops, and **profits**.

(top) With enough water and fertilizer, Iranian farmers can grow peppers and other crops in sand.

Gifts from nature

Wheat, rice, and barley are Iran's major crops. They grow mainly in the foothills and plains of the west and in the north. Other important crops include cotton, lentils, pomegranates, dates, figs, and spices, such as cumin, sumac, and saffron. Saffron is made from the orange-yellow **stigmas** of the crocus plant. The stigmas are handpicked, dried, and used to flavor food and dye cloth.

The climate in the Elburz and Zagros Mountains is ideal for growing almonds, walnuts, pears, and pomegranates. Pistachios, grown in south-central Iran, are a major export. Tea is grown and processed in factories on the Caspian plain, honey is collected from beehives in the northcentral city of Qom, and silk is harvested from silkworm cocoons in most northern and eastern provinces. To make silk, the cocoons are soaked in boiling water and cleaned with a mixture of ash and water. Then, they are dyed and spun into thread, ready to be used for knitting or weaving.

(below) Rice grown in paddies near the Caspian Sea has a hearty, nutty flavor.

Raising livestock

Farmers and herders in Iran farm chickens and raise sheep, goats, cattle, horses, water buffalo, and mules. Most of the country's livestock is raised in the Zagros foothills in the northwest, the Elburz Mountains in the north, and the region of Sistan, in the east. The animals are raised for their meat, milk, wool, and hides, and are used as pack animals.

Catch of the day

Sturgeon, shrimp, trout, and salmon are among the fish caught in the waters in and around Iran. The south shore of the Caspian Sea is known as Iran's "Caviar Coast." Caviar is the roe, or eggs, of the female beluga sturgeon, a fish that can weigh up to one ton (900 kilograms) and live 100 years. Caviar is eaten on crackers or toast, or used as a garnish. It is a rare and expensive treat that is mostly exported. Iran has two large government-run factories that produce half of the world's caviar, although production has recently decreased because pollution in the Caspian Sea has affected the crop.

(above) Many nomadic peoples, including some Qashqai, herd sheep and other livestock.

(below) To make caviar, processors cut open sturgeon to remove the roe. Then, they pass the roe through a fine mesh screen to remove fat or bits of tissue.

⚒ From Iran to the world ⚒

Iran exports many goods to other parts of the world. Foods, such as dried fruits, sugar, and sesame oil, as well as automobiles, appliances, rubber products, steel, and medicines and medical supplies are produced in Iran and sold to many different countries.

Petroleum and natural gas

Iran's main industries are the petroleum and natural gas industries. Petroleum, which is also called crude oil, is a dark-colored liquid that is used to make fuel for vehicles and airplanes. Oil products are also used in plastics, paints, medicines, and fertilizers which are added to soil to help it produce better crops. Natural gas is a flammable mixture of **hydrocarbon** gases found in rock. It provides energy for furnaces, stoves, and other appliances.

(left) ZamZam Cola is made in a factory in Tehran. The drink is named after a spring in the Muslim holy city of Mecca in Saudi Arabia.

(top) The Iran Khodro Industrial Group, based in Tehran, manufactures cars, vans, buses, and trucks that are exported to other Middle Eastern countries.

(above) An oil refinery operating in Tehran.

Extracting oil and gas

The country's rich petroleum and natural gas deposits are located mainly in the southwestern province of Khuzestan and offshore, in the Persian Gulf. Pumps extract petroleum and natural gas from wells, and pipelines carry them to refineries where they are processed, or have their impurities removed. Today, Iran is one of the world's top producers of both petroleum and natural gas.

Other buried treasures

Iran has one of the world's largest reserves of copper, a type of metal. Copper is most often used to make wire for outdoor power lines, home wiring, and electrical machinery. Iran also has valuable deposits of coal, used to create electric power; gold and silver, used to make jewelry and other decorative items; and tin, used to make cans and containers. Marble and alabaster mined in Iran are used for construction, while gemstones, such as amber, lapis lazuli, turquoise, topaz, emerald, and sapphire, are used to make jewelry.

Traditional crafts

Iranian artisans create beautiful handiworks, including woven carpets, tiles, pottery, copperware, brassware, glass, leather goods, and woodwork. Today, some crafts are made by machines in factories, but the most precious pieces are made by hand and take months or even years to complete. Iranian artisans often train for years as apprentices to master craftspeople before they can join a guild. A guild is an organization that ensures the quality of its members' work and protects their interests.

Environmental issues

In its 1979 **constitution**, Iran promised to care for the environment, but years of war with Iraq and trade restrictions left Iran with little money to spend on environmental protection. Air pollution in industrial cities, such as Tehran, Isfahan, and Kerman, is an increasing problem. Factory and vehicle fumes often make people ill with nausea, headaches, and coughing. Oil spills and damaged pipelines in the Persian Gulf have seriously affected water quality and devastated fish and waterfowl species. Clearcutting, or the cutting down of all trees in one area at one time, and **overgrazing** have created barren areas of land that quickly become dry deserts.

Recently, some of Iran's government agencies have created programs to reduce air and noise pollution. In 2004, Iran's Department of the Environment set noise limits for factories, airports, and vehicles. The Air Quality Control Company, in Tehran, monitors pollution from factories and vehicles, as well as fuel usage. Older vehicles are being replaced by newer ones with better exhaust filters that release less pollution. New subway lines are expected to ease traffic on big city streets, so there will be less air pollution from cars.

🏛 Animals rare and wild 🏛

There are more than 100 mammal species in Iran, many of which have adapted to the country's harsh climate. The lush vegetation of the Caspian region provides cover for red deer, cheetahs, and wolves. Twenty-one bat species live inside Iran's damp, warm *qanats*. The Iranian crocodile, or *gandar*, lives in the southeastern region of Baluchistan, in deep, slow-moving rivers, as well as marshes and lakes. This animal was once hunted for its olive-green skin, which was used to make leather. The Iranian crocodile is now threatened by drought and the destruction of its habitat, or area where it lives.

(right) Asiatic cheetahs have black marks that run from the sides of their eyes and down their noses to their mouths. These marks help keep the sun out of the cheetahs' eyes as they hunt.

(top) Migrating birds, including flamingos, spend winters in the islands of the Persian Gulf.

(above) Frog-eye geckos burrow in the sand of Iran's deserts, coming out at night to catch insects to eat.

Desert animals

Iran's desert mammals, such as jackals and rabbits, survive in high temperatures with little water or food. The Iranian fat-tailed sheep has a tail that weighs up to 30 pounds (14 kilograms). The tail stores fat that sustains the sheep in areas with little grass for grazing. Animals such as lizards spend their days in cool burrows, and then venture out at night to lap dew from rocks.

Mountain wildlife

The Elburz and Zagros Mountains are home to frogs, tortoises, lizards, and salamanders, as well as many snake species, including boas and vipers. Vipers have long, hollow fangs filled with venom, or poison, that they use to kill their **prey**. They fold the fangs back into their mouths when they are not needed. **Predators** such as wolves, leopards, bears, and hyenas also live

in the mountain woods, preying on such species as wild boars, wild goats, and gazelles. Wild boars are good swimmers with sharp tusks, which they use to defend themselves against predators and to dig for roots in the ground.

Endangered and extinct animals

Many animals in Iran are endangered, and some, such as the Asiatic lion and Caspian tiger, are already **extinct**. Wild animals are endangered by hunting and habitat destruction, which occurs when humans cut trees, reroute waterways, or construct buildings and roads where animals live.

Iran's Department of the Environment works to protect wildlife and habitats with the help of a series of laws. Sanctuaries such as the Bakhtegan Wildlife Refuge in Fars province, the Turan Protected Area in Semnan province, and the Golestan National Park on the Caspian plain provide a safe home for swans, pheasants, deer, Asiatic cheetahs, and other endangered species.

(left) The onager, or Persian wild ass, is a swift animal related to the donkey. It lives in the dry kavir regions, feeding on herbs, grass, and bushes. In recent years, over-hunting has caused the onager to become nearly extinct.

🏛 Glossary 🏛

aquifer A layer of underground rock able to store large amounts of water

archaeologist A person who studies the past by looking at buildings and artifacts

artifact An object made and used by an earlier culture

caravan A group of travelers or traders journeying together, often for safety reasons

constitution A set of rules, laws, or customs of a government or any other institution

descendant A person who can trace his or her family roots to a certain family or group

dynasty A family or group of rulers in power for a long time

economy A country's system of organizing and managing its businesses, industries, and money

empire A group of countries or territories under one ruler or government

evaporation A process whereby a liquid is changed into a gas

export An item sold to another country

extinct No longer in existence, as with dinosaurs

fertile Able to produce abundant crops or vegetation

foundation The part of a building that supports it

hydrocarbon Containing the chemical elements hydrogen and carbon

irrigation A system of supplying land with water for growing crops

latitude The distance north or south of the equator, measured in degrees

mangrove A tropical tree that is held high above the water by its tangled roots

mineral A naturally occurring, non-living substance obtained through mining

mosque A sacred building in which Muslims worship

nomadic Moving from season to season in search of food and water

overgrazing The grazing, or feeding, of animals for too long in the same place

pilgrimage Relating to a religious journey to a sacred place

plateau An area of flat land that is higher than the surrounding land

predator An animal that kills and eats other animals

prey An animal hunted by another animal for food

profit Money left over after all business costs have been paid

refugee A person who is forced to leave his or her home because of danger

reservoir A body of water that has been collected and stored for future use

semi-nomadic Living and growing crops in one place for part of the year, and traveling to hunt and gather food for the other part

stigma The part of a plant where pollen is deposited

🏛 Index 🏛